DEEP

A collection of short poems

By

Keith Hearn

Writing poetry is very like writing short stories

Hopefully the poems will enable others to connect with at least one of my poems

I hope I will inspire others to write

My book is dedicated to my children Sara-Ann and Paul

To my grandchildren Caitlin, Chloe, Josh and Bella

*Always follow your dreams
a dream never goes away, even if it is
hidden for many years, it will be
locked away in the mind until it
surfaces once again*

Be Inspired

*Never let others put you off aiming
high in life*

Be creative and enjoy the experience

DEEP

FEELINGS

*How fickle other people's feelings for
one another can be*

*I seem to be unable to gauge a woman's
feelings towards me*

*I say one thing and get a completely
different reaction to the one I was
expecting*

Who am I to argue

I am only a man, who knows no better

*Oh, joy to live life with the female of
the species*

HAPPY

Summer is such a happy time of the
year

The sun seems to bring out the best in
others

People seem to be so much kinder and
friendlier towards others

So many people smile so much more
during the summer months

Happiness seems to be the order of the
day

The summer months are so much more
of a relaxed time of the year

DEEP

*Children can be seen running about
outside without a care in the world*

Such joyous times

FLOWER

The flower stood in solitude within the garden, in full bloom desperately trying to attract a suiter to her gift of life

Each morning she would ensure she looked the best in the garden

Once the sun is at its zenith, the flower would look so pretty, its colours looking so bright and enticing

The flowers petals were bright orange and glowed in the light

The flower seemed to be trying so hard to attract the many bees to her

enticing pollen and her life giving
nectar
Without the bees in the world everyone
is affected, without the flower and the
humble bee, humanity would soon die
out

Mother nature is the mother of all
living things on the planet

Without nature to provide it bounty,
we are in danger of risking our very
exitance on the planet

EARLY MORNING

Waking up early morning is such a joy
on a glorious summers morn

Watching the sun breaking through
the early morning haze and mist

Birds chirping outside, announcing the
start of the day ahead

The dew laying on the grass forming a
shimmering carpet of water, waiting
to be burnt off by the mornings sun

Slugs slowly moving out of the of the
glare of sun's rays, before shriveling up
and drying out, or becoming a tasty
morsel for a bird's breakfast

DEEP

Such a beautiful feeling on a summers morn

FIELDS

The farmer's fields full of ripening crops ready for harvesting

Full of amazing hues of green's and red's

The crops swaying on the slight breeze on a late lazy summers afternoon

A combine harvester can be heard in the distance, a plume of dust billowing from behind the combine

Birds are in flight avoiding being sucked up into the machinery of the combine, the birds landing behind the combine pecking at the seed left behind

DEEP

The buzzards are circling high above
the combine waiting for any field mice
or shrews to make a dash across the
naked ground lain waste by the
combine

Kestrels can be seen hovering above
the field, there and their wings
flapping to keeping the birds in the sky

The rooks can be seen high in the sky
dueling with the buzzards

So much action in such a small area

Man, and nature trying to feed their
own species in very diverse ways
all with the same goal

<u>*TIME*</u>

The seasons seem to fly by the older we become

As soon as spring arrives then it no sooner summer arrives with its lovely weather

As soon as we become used to the summer and its bounty of goodness it disappears and just is a memory

Then bang it is the colder months of autumn with its many colours, the leaves turn red, brown and yellow and begin to fall to the ground preparing for the wintery months

DEEP

*As soon as the leaves have disappeared
from the trees then it is the winter
with its dark mornings and even
darker evenings*

*Jack frost will soon arrive and cover
the ground with frost and ice*

*And maybe there will be a covering of
snow covering the fields in a blanket of
snow*

LOCAL

Lounging in the local pub, watching people coming and going

So many different people arrive in every shape and size

Some are happy and some look so sad

People with their own personal stories of life

Some with happy stories and some with heartbreaking stories

Once inside the pub they seem to become more open and so much happier

DEEP

Lunch soon finishes and the pub
gradually empties

People disperse with their thoughts
and memories

SUMMER

On a hot summers day, it makes
everyone feel so good about themselves
and the world around them

The feeling makes life's troubles seem so
far away and a distant memory

Watching the bees fly into the centre of
a bright coloured flower, the pace of
life seems so much slower

The colours of the garden stand out in
all their glory

Life soon interrupts and life is soon
back to normality

<u>*WORDS*</u>

*Words can be so much deadlier than
the sword*

*Words do not kill, but at the same time
they can sentence a person to death in
more ways than one*

Words can seem frivolous and hollow

*Some people long for the right words to
be uttered by another*

Just one kind word that is all it takes

Love

*People can be cut in half by harmful
words*

A person can be made the loneliest person by the utterances of the wrong words

Words place people in boxes for life

Words can bring governments crashing down

Freedom to speak out can worry those in power

Freedom is such a powerful word

A SOLDIERS TALE

In peacetime, a soldier is tolerated by others in society

The local pubs fling open their doors for a soldier's custom and pay packet

In peacetime soldiers argue and fight between themselves

Once a soldier is needed by their nation, the whole nation stands solidly behind its military

A soldier in the field sees things no one else can ever dream of witnessing

Once the heat of the battle is over, the soldier returns home, maybe physically unscathed, but the battle continues within the mind the nightmares never ending

Some are unlucky and return with the physical scars of war including the dreaded nightmares

And there are those who never return to stand proudly with their comrades

All we can do is to always remember them

To never forget their ultimate sacrifice to our nation

<u>WINCHESTER CATHEDRAL</u>

Winchester cathedral on an autumn morning is such a sight to behold

The calm and still atmosphere takes one back to a bygone era and the mind drifts away back to a time when the city was truly a historical maze

The sense of longevity surrounding the cathedral, is a vision of beauty

There have been centuries of people entering the cathedral for personal prayer

It is a place of sanctuary if ever needed

*On this morning, the rays of sunlight
are streaming through the branches of
the trees within the cathedral grounds*

*The stonework of the cathedral is
bathed in the autumn light making the
cathedral glow*

*The observer cannot help but be moved
by the colossal scale of the building*

*From the outside the building there
isn't any colour only the red paint on
the main doors*

*The towers are cast against the wisps
of white cloud*

<u>*SAXON*</u>

Set in the grounds of the great Saxon church, the Norman cathedral now stands it is such a mystical feeling, it is a sense of true ancient history

It is a place where one tries to imagine who may have previously walked the same grounds hundreds of years ago

To think of the time the great Saxon kings and lords had gathered in the same spot

The great Saxon hall has long disappeared to be replaced by the grand Norman building

ALONE

I see so many happy people going about their own business

Some of them are alone and many with others by their side

Here am I sat on a park bench, alone, only with my thoughts as company

Thinking to myself will it be yet another year alone with only my thoughts as company

Maybe if I gave up on my dream of finding someone in my life

That special person may turn up!!

AUTUMN SUN

The autumn sunlight is streaming
through the morning mist

Bathing the lush green lawn with a
golden hue

People are laughing and chatting ten
to the dozen

The scene is different to a cold winters
morn

The sun streams through the leaves
that now cover the trees

The lull before the cold winters
mornings arrive

THE OLD SOLDIERS RESTING PLACE

*The old headstones scattered around
the cathedral grounds are full of
symbols of a bygone age*

*A few old soldier's headstones protrude
from the grass*

*What kind of stories have these men
taken to their graves?*

Stories of far off lands and wars

*To then come home to the mundane life
of a soldier in barracks*

*Just like a soldier's life today, for a
soldier nothing ever changes*

SEASONS

Autumn is upon the land clearing the
way for the cold winter months

Autumn ensures the leaves on the trees
have been laid bare

Ensuring winter can freeze nature and
to slow the pace of growth until the
new season arrives

To allow the magic of spring and to
encourage mother nature to grow once
more

Then for the summer months to
explode and provide the fruits of
nature's bounty

CITIES

Childhood of living in an industrial shipping city, in the north of England

It is a far cry to the city I would call my home

My city in the north is the city I have travelled the world, I have never forgotten the city I was born in

I now live in a Roman city far from the hustle and bustle of the north

My roots are steeped in the culture of the north

The smoke and fog drifting across the river Mersey are memories that have been chiseled on my mind

The Roman city has no industry and is sometimes covered in the smog from car fumes, and not the smog of heavy industry, which is a modern curse

FUTURE

It is no good looking back to the past

To move forward one must look to the future and not the past

The future has so much more to give

Looking to the past makes one stick to the past and what could have been

The future encourages a person to grow and to develop

RELATIONSHIPS

Why do people self-destruct

They cannot be apart but together they
are like a match setting the blue touch
paper alight

They can only live in an explosive
relationship

But they cannot live apart

<u>*VIEWS*</u>

It is a world where we can change for the better

There are powers to be who do not wish for things to be changed for the better, as it suites their purpose for things in the world to remain as they are

Mine might be a cynical view, but it is one, over time, is growing stronger

The world is becoming a smaller place to live in

People with a world view are very few and far between

<u>*LOVING EYES*</u>

Eyes are the gateways to the soul

Looking deep is when two people cannot see what is happening around them

They are in a trance like state with one another other

Each day they cannot see what is happening on their own doorstep

They only have eyes for one another

Love can be deep and blinding

<u>*DARE*</u>

Dare I dream of what could be

Or am I getting too carried away as usual

Am I scaring you away?

Do I come across as needy?

I just don't seem to be able to control my feelings

Hopefully you will stay and see this through

DEEP

FEELINGS

*I haven't felt this way about someone
for many years*

*There is something that tells me, I
think this is so right*

I don't know how you feel about this

So far you haven't brushed me aside

*I am wary about all of this because it
is so new and different*

*For once I seem to be able to breath
and have something to think about*

Who knows what the future may hold

37

A BEAUTIFUL DAY

It started with a comment
online to a professor
requesting people to star in a
music video
My reply to Professor Green's
message was to inform his team
that I was far too old to star in
his video

Out of the blue you replied "us
oldies must stick together", how
I smiled

I know you enjoy the sight of
the many different hues of the
autumn leaves, the bright reds,
yellow and deep greens of the
falling leaves drifting in the air
to gentle fall to the ground,
covering the common in a
blanket of colour

DEEP

*Your chirping friend fly's
around your garden, puffing
his bright red breast for all to
see, darting from place to place,
he keeps you company*

*Your loyal dogs keep you
company and show you their
undying love for you*

*I like the way you post pictures
of the coffee shops in and
around where you live, I find
you so interesting*

*Your reply to my message to
the professor has opened your
world to so many others*

*Thank you for allowing me to
begin to get to know you*

KINDNESS

There is something that comes across about you time and time again and it is your kindness

You are passionate about the things that matter to you

I don't wish to suffocate you and to push you away

I am so passionate about the things that matter to me

My passion runs into so many other aspects of my life

I am true to my word

EXPOSURE

To see you on the front page of the newspaper was so amazing

You were protesting at the death of a young woman who rode her bicycle on a busy London road

Oh, how you cared for the young woman and what had happened to her

The roads in London are teeming with vehicles

In the Newspaper's photograph, you look serene your long hair cascading down your back, and with your devoted dog by your side

DEEP

You are dressed in black

I can see your olive skin highlighted by
the dark colour of your top

People are sat or lying on the road to
register their outrage at yet another
death on London's hectic roads

How caring and passionate you are

Such a very special person

DEEP

WOODS

The light breaks through the ancient
wood

Shafts of light are cascading onto the
forest floor

Lighting the way along the ancient
footpath

To the left is the old Roman road is
running parallel and as straight as an
arrow

The mind plays tricks, almost taking
the person walking the footpath, back
to ancient times

DEEP

*Trying hard to imagine a Roman
Army marching along the road*

*The footpath is sunken below an
embankment running parallel with an
ancient highway*

*Alone in the wood one can imagine
times gone past*

Within the mists of ancient history

A DISTANT FIELD

His bones lie under soil in a far off
foreign field

He has lain alone in the field for a
millennium or more

His skin and uniform have long been
stripped from his body

His bones have been stained by the
efforts of the soil, the soil has hidden
him from the world for far too long

His life was far cut down far too soon

When alive the furthest he had ever
travelled was to the local town on
market day

His education was limited; at the time of enlistment he could not drink or vote

At the age of sixteen he had lied about his age and had enlisted into the Army

At the age seventeen he had been to laid to rest in the field at the same place he was killed in action

There was no one to morn his passing, no one to bury him, mother nature took care of him and laid him in her bosom

He has lain alone for so long; his comrades are laid to rest in a graveyard close across from the same

DEEP

*field they were felled so many years
ago*

Together in life and death

SOME THINGS NEVER CHANGE

A soldier's lot is the same today as it
had been hundreds of years ago

For the infantry fighting on the
ground today, sat in his slit trench it is
the same as soldiers had done going
back hundreds of years

It is only the technology of today's
Army where the battlefield has
changed

A soldier of today who is shot or blown
to pieces on the plains of the desert,
will be flown to a field hospital in life
saving time

DEEP

*To be flown from the theatre of war to
a major hospital in the UK*

*The longest battle a soldier will face
are the battles he will fight each day
will be within the mind itself*

THE POPPY

I find for some unknown reason this year the poppy has become a political symbol

And for that reason, the poppy has taken on a greater significance

The silliness has extended to the football pitch

There are those who would like to ban the wearing of the poppy

People have lost sight of the reason why the poppy is worn

To refer to the wearing of the poppy as a political symbol is a slur on the fallen

and the thousands who have served
and live with their injuries, both
physical and mental scars

May the poppy forever remain as a
symbol of the nation's fallen

How the wearing of the poopy has been
distorted in today's cynical world

ICY COLD

The winter weather is once again about to descend on the countryside

As soon as the frost and snow has lain on the ground the land will remain dormant for many months

All of nature's creatures will enter a period of hibernation and will not appear until the warmer weather begins to break in the spring sunshine

Food will be scarcer in the cold winter months

The icy wind freezing everything in its path

WHITE STONES ON PARADE

In the midday sun the light shines onto
the white gravestones, the stones are
lined up in neat rows

They look like they are still on parade
at Horse Guards, Aldershot or
Pirbright, each stood to attention

There are thousands of white
gravestones, they are a visible and
poignant symbol of a lost generation

The fallen had fought a war to end all
wars, to enable future generations to
live in peace, they paid the ultimate
sacrifice

DEEP

*The sheer scale of death and
destruction is on such an industrial
scale*

*The great war took healthy men and
spewed out dead and broken men no
one was spared*

*Who will remember them after a
hundred years' have passed*

*At the going down of the sun and in
the morning, we will remember them*

Quote Poem For the Fallen by Laurence Binyon

A CHANGING WORLD

The world is politically changing and so many people are holding their breath wondering what the future will hold for them

The people of Britain have been given a vote regarding the Referendum to leave or remain in the European Union

The vote was on the 23rd of June 2016 the politicians must have felt safe in the knowledge the result of the Referendum would be a foregone conclusion

Most of people voted by a slim margin to leave the European Union

Its seems as though the so called political elite are trying to usurp the will of the people

Many politicians seem to be dragging their feet to carry out the will of the people

During 2016 America, have since chosen their future leader, and at the same time the political elite of America have been caught off balance by the result

Russia has its own leader, a leader who will make the bear more powerful, and not the teddy bear of the recent past

The people of Britain need a Churchillian type of leader once more hopefully someone who will make the lion roar once more

LIFES FAULT LINES

No one knows how life will play out

Life has a habit of turning one's world upside down

As soon as it happens nothing can ever be the same again

Things can never be able to slot back into place, just as though nothing had ever happened

When life has been disturbed along the fault line, nothing will be the same again

Fault lines have never been designed to just slot exactly back into the same place

Life never runs smoothly and we must adapt and to try to make a situation better

Life can change so quickly, just like the blink of an eye

It is what we do with our lives to make things better that counts

<u>*SEASONS*</u>

The seasons are rapidly changing from the warmth of summer

Headlong into cold autumn days

Very soon it will be the depths of winter and the cold dark nights

The winter months aren't everyone's favorite time of year

For I can't wait for the first signs of spring

Natures natural cycle soon grinds to a standstill during the winter months

The odd days of snow covered fields is such a beautiful sight, it seems so short lived

DEEP

I cannot wait for the wintery days to come to an end, it just isn't my cup of tea

<u>*THOUGHTS OF YOU*</u>

*You came from nowhere and knocked
me off my feet*

I didn't see you coming!!

*You have sent my imagination into
overdrive*

*I have tantalising thoughts of what if?
can it be real*

Will there be a future in it?

*Can I ever have what others have and
take for granted*

*Could you be the one who brings
happiness into my life?*

*Possibly I look too deeply into the
matters of the heart, and things that
aren't there in the first place*

PRINCIPLE

I feel so lucky to have my children in my life

Our road has been very rocky to say the least

From those early days of fighting to be united and together

You have given me the gift of so many grandchildren

Life seems to go around in circles

Maybe our lives have gone full circle and it is someone else's turn to jump onto the circle of life

My love for you knows no bounds

<u>DARKNESS</u>

The darkness descends like a curtain
blocking the light

There is no warning or any indication
of the forthcoming prevailing darkness

There doesn't seem to be a way of
escaping from the darkness

The darkness permeates throughout a
person's daily life

There seems to be only one way to
escape from the darkness and the
weight of the dread poured upon one's
shoulders

<u>*EASY*</u>

I have enjoyed messaging over the weeks

I instantly realised I had overdone things as per usual

I initially thought that you were different and would accept the way I am

I can be far too passionate and overbearing at times, it is in my nature

I realise even you have become tired of my messages

Maybe remaining on my own is the best thing for everyone concerned

It may make life so much easier

Easy is easy, there are no complications or ant commitment to another

No nothing

It's so easy?

<u>MOANER</u>

The customers at the pub were sat eating and drinking and enjoying one another's company

In walked a man who had such a loud voice it pierced the atmosphere and the ambiance of the pub

He began to walk around the bar to find a place to sit at

He was ensuring he could find a spot for his dog, a kind member of staff found a spot so he could sit anywhere apart from the restaurant area

He eventually found a suitable table, he then proceeded to complain about a chair, he mentioned how rough it looked, he became louder and louder

A more acceptable chair was soon found, he then went on to complain about the chair having an unacceptable cushion

A cushion was soon found and duly placed on the chair

He decided to sit on a different chair

He came across as a bit of a moaner and he was complaining for the sake of it

He seemed to be the sort of person who wouldn't be happy about anything

Someone who liked the sound of his own voice

NEARLY GONE FOREVER

How refreshing to see you are back?

I thought you had disappeared forever

It has been such a peculiar feeling not being able to be in contact with you

I don't know what it is about you

I know my outlook on life has changed for the better

I know life isn't too good for you right now, it is only you who can sort things out for yourself

I am always around if you need me

<u>*COCKNEY SPARROW*</u>

*I don't know who you are we have
never met*

*I have heard your voice and you seem
very nice, a cockney sparrow*

I always seem to have too much to say

*I don't know when to stop rabbiting
away, it is a bad trait of mine*

*You on the other hand are very
reserved*

*Whatever you say is so profound and
to the point*

DARKNESS AND LIGHT

Now that the dark nights have
arrived, it is a time of the year that I
don't look forward to

I wish the wintery days away and
think of the first days of spring

The first signs of spring are when the
shoots of the daffodil break through the
soil

For me it is a welcome sign, to me it
means winter is over for yet another
year

I detest coming home to a dark and
cold house

DEEP

As soon spring arrives the house is so warm and full of light and most welcoming

<u>*RELECTIONS*</u>

It will soon be the day I will be donning my suit and wearing my medals to pay homage to the many fallen

For me it is a proud and poignant morning, it is a sad day time to reflect on comrades who are no longer with us

It is a day of Remembrance and reflection

The cathedral will be packed with many people also to remember and to reflect on those who are no longer with us, they are in all our thoughts

DEEP

*In attendance, will be many old
soldiers wearing their medals
resplendent on their jackets*

*The various medals on display are a
living history of the nation's history*

*Each will have their own memories of
loved one past and present*

They are never forgotten

FESTIVE

*Already people are talking about
Christmas it is only October*

*Christmas seems so far away weeks
away, not so long at all*

*Christmas can be such a double-edged
sword, between those who want for
nothing and those who have nothing*

*Christmas isn't about the materialistic
things*

*The story of Christmas is about the
birth of the baby Jesus*

*It has nothing to do with a
materialistic world*

PEACE AT LAST

*He served in a far off foreign land, he
lies in a foreign field far from loved
ones*

*He was in a patrol wading through a
sunken stream surrounded by an oasis
of green enclosed within a desert, so
hot and dry where nothing ever grew*

*His patrol was pinned down by enemy
sniper fire*

*At some stage during the engagement
he was shot in the leg and the pain was
horrendous*

*After a while he felt the pain subsiding
it was replaced by a feeling of*

*numbness the soldier couldn't feel his
leg. He was sliding into a deep sleep*

*He could just make out his comrades
shaking him and shouting at him to
stay with them*

He wasn't responding to their efforts

Everything felt so peaceful

*He eventually slipped away and died
in a foreign land so far from home*

*He died alongside his "mates" he
wasn't on his own. He was doing what
he thought was right and just*

<u>WHY ME</u>

I sometimes think to myself, why me

*Maybe I am selfish and maybe I have
put myself first before others*

*I have most things in life, there is one
thing that I do not have and that is
having someone in my life*

*I feel I have so much to give to
someone*

*In life, it takes two to make a
relationship*

DESTRUCTION

The natural world has one aim and the aim is to survive on this wonderful and amazing planet

The natural world has a battle against the destruction man is inflicting on the planet

Humans are placing everything in jeopardy including the planet itself

Nations are jousting for supremacy of the planet, creating even more lethal ways of destroying great swathes of the planet

A great many areas of the planet have been poisoned and are under constant bombardment, man is on a continuous quest to rape the planet of its natural resources

Man, seems to want to kill other members of our species in their thousands and without any remorse or thought

There will be a time when it will be too late to pull away from the dark abyss

There will come a time when mother nature will take her revenge

PASSION

I have found you so interesting and mentally stimulating

Even though my time with you has been so short

You are a person with strong values and passion

I was conscious I was overpowering and stifling

Your passion took you to a sit down protest regarding the killing of cycleilists in London

DEEP

You managed to get yourself on the front cover over a well-known London Newspaper

Live your life to the full and make a difference to others

Loyalty

A soldier is never wanted or needed in peacetime

As soon as the politicians create a situation and cannot resolve an issue soldiers are then sent in to sort out a politician's have created

A cry soon goes out to send in the troops, when the politicians have lied

Once the soldiers are home the politicians start to lay blame at the feet of the soldiers

The politicians send in the blood hounds to hunt down the men and women of our Armed Forces

*They allow the lawyers to hound the
wounded and the living for carrying
out the politician's work*

*The only people who come out well
during this debacle are the soldiers
themselves*

*The cowards are the politicians and
lawyers who do the politicians bidding*

*War has changed over a period of a
hundred years or so, the military not
only fight an enemy on the
battleground, they fight a new war
when they are back home*

*The military have always remained
loyal to the crown*

The politicians scratch their heads and cannot understand why they can no longer recruit into the Armed Forces?

A WORRIED WORLD

We all live in an age where people are
becoming more and more scared of
speaking out about politics just in case
they may lose their livelihood

Freedom of speech seems to have
become more and more eroded within
the United Kingdom

Is this the new horizon in the United
Kingdom in late 2016?

People are becoming even more
alarmed regarding the states
governing apparatus

How things have changed in the
modern world

There is a feeling the United Kingdom is becoming more like the old era of the USSR

The nations freedom of speech seems to have been severely eroded

The politicians of our sceptered isle have taken their eyes off the people they supposedly represent

DEMOCRATIC ELECTIONS

Today the world has been rocked to the
core by the results of the most powerful
person in the free world

It has felt as though it was some sort of
joke or a nightmare

Time will only tell if he will turn the
world for the better

Here is hoping

No one will know how things will turn
out, until the latest president has been
given time to prove himself

Rightly or wrongly the fate of the
world is in the hands of one person

WHO ARE YOU

I know who I am but who are you

You don't seem to want to allow me into your life

No one in your family or your friends know about me I am the dirty little secret hidden away

I am the opposite and would dearly let you into my world

Who are you and what do you want

Are you hiding a dirty little secret of your own?

I am not angry only frustrated

DEEP

98231213R00050

Made in the USA
Columbia, SC
22 June 2018